Five Steps to
Great Parenting

Five Steps to Great Parenting

Insights and Examples

Tom Rowley

NCP
New City Press
of the Focolare
Hyde Park, New York

Published in the United States by New City Press
202 Comforter Blvd., Hyde Park, NY 12538
www.newcitypress.com
©2014 Tom Rowley

Cover design by Leandro de Leon

Real-Life Stories unless otherwise noted are printed with permission
from various issues of *Living City Magazine*.

A catalog record is available from the Library of Congress.

ISBN 978-1-56548-515-0

Printed in the United States of America

Contents

Step *4*

Step *5*

Introduction

At the beginning of creation there is a man and a woman. God entrusts them with the commandment of mutual love and he invites them to multiply and to use all created things. It is a beautiful image; it is the discovery of the existence of the other and the birth of the family.

Chiara Lubich[1]

*W*ITH VERY FEW EXCEPTIONS, all parents want what is best for their children. They want their children to be happy, healthy, responsible, loving, respectful, courageous, generous, and grateful. In other words, most parents aspire to be *great* parents.

Many of us parents may remember hearing our grandmothers say, "It's harder to raise kids today than it was when I was growing up." Whether this is true or not doesn't really matter because the ultimate task of raising children and maintaining a close-knit family remains in the hands of every parent. We have the gifts for raising our families, and if we have children, we certainly want the best for them in every way.

If it *is* true, however, that it is harder today than before, parents' *active* vigilance is even more necessary. Our role as models becomes much more essential because the world offers many other models — attractive things to get involved in at the expense of building a united family. So many things tend to create little islands within a family that reduce and limit personal interactions.

I remember when our children were young and Nintendo's *Mario Brothers* came out for the first time. That program was so interesting that for several weeks, I found that my children and I sat in front of the TV eating our dinner and challenging each other to master the game. It was indeed fun but what we lost during that time was the wonderful communication we had before when we sat around the table talking over the day, sharing our joys and concerns. We found ourselves completely engrossed in the game and not in each other. Moreover, one member of the family was often left out because my wife, JoAnn, didn't really like the amount of time we spent at the game. For the kids and me, it really seemed like a good thing because we were doing something together. But were we all together?

So many things that seem good have the power of eating away at the unity of the family. The things that all parents want for their children get pushed aside or blurred, leaving gaps between the parents and their children, between the siblings too, and even between the husband and wife.

After speaking with single parents and couples who are raising or who have raised children, I made a list of the chief "enemies" of family life. Here are a few of the things they told me. Most of us have experienced them first-hand: Television; YouTube; online programming; sports programs; work schedule; social media; technology; games; cell phones; friends; dating; and a sense of entitlement.

It would be tempting to demonize these things, but are they bad? We can certainly acknowledge that they can and many times do become distractions for a family, but when put into a structure of well-thought-out priorities, these things can be useful to building up a family.

As a husband of 52 years and a father of five children, I would say that I have tried most of the time to be motivated by my faith and my deep desire to love each member of my family. That is why the primary focus of this little book is love.

One may ask, "But what is love?" Is it a feeling, an emotion? The definition of love that I find most useful is simply this: "putting the needs of the other ahead of my own." This means putting the other in first place. Loving means adhering to the Golden Rule, "Do to others as you would have them do to you." Our pastor refers to love as "the opportunity to seek the good of the other above our own needs."

Each member of my family has a different personality, and thus different needs and ways of thinking. It is amazing that children brought up in essentially the same atmosphere can be so different. Therefore, I try to treat each person in the family in a way that expresses personal love and acceptance.

Every family has common characteristics as well as being very different. We have known families with very difficult challenges that become stronger because of them. On the other hand, we have known families that have collapsed over similar challenges. It very much depends on whether a family is built on solid loving relationships between its members.

It is our hope that the 5 steps in this small book will help readers examine their own families in order to discover in them what is true, good, and beautiful. With these steps we hope that parents will build better and stronger relationships among themselves and their children. We hope this will provide a firm foundation for your children as they grow up in an alluring world so full of distractions where hearts are hardened and feelings are dulled.

When parents become true models and when love is maintained over everything else, a family becomes a living witness to others. This is what great parenting is based on. They will demonstrate what family life can become. The world needs strong families based on love because we are living at a time in which parenting and family values have become weak and distorted.

Let's see if it is possible to enjoy what the world has to offer in a new way, a way that helps our children navigate through the many obstacles that distract them from understanding how to build lasting and strong relationships in their family and with others. Let's take these 5 steps together and discover how they lead to greater parenting.

Acknowledgements

I would like to thank the Schaff, Moreau and Ariza families along with Karen Armstrong who graciously gave time to be interviewed as a contribution to this work. Without your insights I couldn't have done it. I would also like to thank my pastor, Fr. Lockey for his support and encouragement.

I dedicate this book to all families.

Step 1
Love One Another

Devised by God as a masterpiece of love, the family is able to inspire the guidelines that can contribute to changing tomorrow's world. In fact, if we look at the family, if we were to take an X-ray of it, we would discover enormous and precious values, which if projected and applied to all of humanity have the potential to transform it into one big family.

Chiara Lubich[2]

*W*HERE DO CHILDREN LEARN about caring for others? Where do they find that every human being has an inherent dignity? Who instills in children the awareness to be grateful and loving to one another? The answers to these questions are found in the way a great parent lives the following four principles.

The first is through *example*. Children learn most from what their parents model. From a very early age a child witnesses and imitates how parents live their lives. Our son had a job that required him to wake up early in the morning before school. He took his responsibility seriously by waking up on his own at 4:30 every morning. JoAnn set an example by getting up before him so he wouldn't be alone. It was amazing how that small sacrifice on her part stimulated conversations and deepened their relationship to the point that he still refers to those times some 15 years later.

The second way is through *practice*. Parents who consistently share stories with their children about moral choices they've made during the week are helping them to see that putting love into action is a choice made many times during the week. Sharing our personal experiences is one of the best ways to help our children learn how to treat people in their own lives. We can share an opinion and people can take issue with it, but they are less likely to object when we share our personal experience.

Thirdly, we can see that *the words parents use* to explain and justify what they do have the effect of demonstrating the care they have for their children. Their actions match the words: "I love you." Children learn that loving the other is fulfilling and this helps them to become themselves in the truest sense.

A friend shared this example:

> One day, my four-year-old came home from school to say, "Every time we do something at school, this boy Joey needs his project to be the best. We all drew pictures today, and he kept saying his was the best. And he does that all the time." I asked my daughter if she could think of a way to show this boy love. She couldn't. So, I said, "Try this. Tomorrow, if he does something and insists that it's the BEST, tell him you really like it, you really think it's nice." I explained to her that if she tries to find something she really likes about his work, he would know that she loves him just like God loves him. She came home the next day to tell me, "I can't believe it. Today, he finished a math project and said his was the best, and I told him it was really good and that I liked how he made the colors different. You were totally right. He was really happy. Then when we did the reading project, he didn't say his was the best!"

Finally, and this may be something that we overlook even in our sincerest efforts to engage in great parenting, love demands *quality time* spent with our children. I once heard that the average amount of quality time fathers spend with their children per day is less than 15 minutes. In my experience, this has never fulfilled the needs of anyone in my family, including mine. Quality time means time engaged with the family through sharing, playing, and being present in order to reinforce the value of each member of the family. It requires us, as family members, to rethink and reprioritize how we spend our time at home.

I tried hard to leave the work-related problems that I encountered during the day at the door of my home, so I could be present to JoAnn and my children. This was not an easy thing to do, but I made an effort to let go mentally of what happened at work because the most joy-filled part of my day was being with those that I love the most. This meant giving undivided attention to each member with eye contact and with touch. It means telling JoAnn and my children, not necessarily through words, (although that's great too) but through the time spent with them that they were important and very much loved.

So let's explore three simple aspects of love in family life that can influence our children in lasting and profound ways.

Love demands that we recognize and respect that each person we encounter is unique.

I remember learning this the hard way. As a newlywed husband more than 50 years ago, I could never understand why when JoAnn shared a problem we would end up disagreeing after I offered her the solution. One day I think I got it! She is a woman with an ability to solve her own problems. What she needed was someone to listen so that she could think the problem through. The same holds true for our children. They learn problem solving through having the freedom to share with us without fear of judgment or reprimand. They, like JoAnn, just need someone to understand by listening and perhaps offering guidance when it's asked for. We always will have the chance to model appropriate responses, rather than immediate reactions, to our children whenever they share their concerns, problems, joys, and even sufferings with us. When this happens, they can clearly see that our actions match what we say.

How unique and powerful this is when we begin to put the needs of the other in the place of our own needs. Our children begin to see and understand that a parent's love can really be consistent and meaningful.

Love generates positive relationships between generations.

Often there seems to be a chasm between parents and children. Usually it is called the "Generation Gap." Parents often fail to identify with the way their children solve problems, how they organize their lives, the way they communicate, and even how they show their feelings.

At one time I thought that it was so easy to tell my children that there was a better way to deal with the challenges that life presented. After all, I have "been there, done that." I found however, that this approach generally produced friction and the repeated comment, "Dad you just don't understand." That was true, I did not understand that to love my children meant to give them the opportunity to make discoveries, to feel the pain of not succeeding, and to grow into independent people. I had to love them where they were. I had to make their concerns my own. In doing this, I understood that they didn't need a problem solver; they needed the chance to work the problem out with confidence. They had to trust that their parents were available to help if needed. This took a lot of restraint and practice on my part but over time, the "Generation Gap" disappeared and our trust for one another grew.

Love Heals.

Love is always selfless and always values the needs of the other. It means making the choice to put ourselves in the shoes of the others and to try to see things from their perspectives. I spoke to a single parent who started her day with several things going badly. The first thing was coming into her living room and finding that none of the snack dishes from the previous night had been picked up. Feeling a bit irritated while pouring her coffee, she tipped the pot too far, the top flew off, and coffee went everywhere. At that moment, her daughter handed her some forms that were due that day at school, which her daughter had for over a week. Judgments blurted out in abundance and tensions grew to the point of an "explosion of emotion." The damage took its toll. The children went sadly off to school and mom spent a good part of the morning lamenting the fact that she had "blown it."

At the end of the day, the children came home where mom apologized and told the kids she loved them and that she should have spoken to them in a different way and taken the time to listen to their needs. In turn, the daughter apologized for holding on to the forms that should have been presented the night before when everyone had the time. They also promised to remember to clean up after they had their snacks at night. Peace in the family was reestablished.

Our children learn that the best way to experience how love heals is to make the choice to love the person they are with at that moment through listening without judgment or without jumping to conclusions and offering solutions that are not asked for. This is very often a family member and the relationship is always reestablished. Our children learn compassion and patience, and they develop skills in how to love their neighbors.

Real-Life Story
Folding with My Son[3]

My 9-year-old son's room is usually messy. Even though he is supposed to pick up his clothes every night, he finds this "chore" painful. One day, while he was at school, I went into his room to look for something. When I attempted to open his two drawers, I couldn't. They were stuffed with clothes! I took them all out and put them in a pile on the floor. How many times had I told him to fold or hang up his clothes!

When he came home and walked in his room, he was very upset. I was not surprised when he began to yell at me, telling me that he was not going to pick them up. We had had this exchange before — in fact, many times before.

This time, however, I thought, "How can I love him?" Trying to put myself in his place I wondered, "Maybe he had had a rough day at school; maybe he was overwhelmed with all those clothes."

I calmly walked into his room and began to fold and hang up his clothes. As I was folding, I asked him how his day had gone. We began to talk. A couple of minutes later, he jumped off his bunk bed to help me. We continued to talk until we put away all of his clothes.

About an hour later, it was time for me to cook dinner. My son came in from playing outside with his friends and began talking to me in the kitchen. This was unusual. At one point, he watched me getting the spaghetti out of the cupboard and asked, "Mom, will you teach me how to make spaghetti?" This was even more unusual. I have prayed for a long time to have a relationship of dialogue with my children.

We were both proud of his spaghetti.

Real-Life Story
The Bag Left Behind[4]

I picked up my daughter from school to take her to her volleyball game. I was happy to be able to support her in something she really liked. Her team won the game, and when we left she was very happy. However, as we were on our way home, she realized that she had left her bag of clothes on the steps of her school. She didn't seem too worried, because she felt they would be right where she left them. But that wasn't the case when we returned to the school. The bag was gone and so were all of her things. Then she remembered that inside the bag, among other things, were a ring given to her by a close family friend, her favorite shirt and pants, and an album full of pictures. She was very upset.

I shared with her about the gospel and how this was an opportunity to live it in a very personal way.

We spoke about what a challenge the gospel offers us. I suggested we think that perhaps the person who took her things needed them more than she did. It seemed to help her.

Later that night, I was looking for a thermal shirt and pants I had just bought that day. I looked all over for them and finally went to my daughter's room to ask her if she knew where they were. She looked up at me with the same look I had given her when her bag was gone. Then she told me that my things were also in the bag that was taken! "Now you can love them too, mom," she said to me.

Step 2
Is the Issue or the Person More Important?
(The little things do count)

If we overcome difficulties, we reach complete fulfillment, total love. A husband and wife share everything and, therefore, there is no room for egoism or holding back something. It is a love that calls for your whole being in all its depth, physical and spiritual. There will always be differences in a family. These differences can be mutual enrichment for every member.

Anna Maria Zanzucchi[5]

ROM AN EARLY AGE, children learn from the example of their parents. Putting in the first place those we love most, is a good start. Often we put those things mentioned in the introduction into first place. For example, when we take the family out for a hamburger, the usual traps await us at the restaurant. The large-screen TV's on every wall showing different sporting events. How hard it is for the family to keep focused on enjoying their time together without getting pulled away from each other and lost in the games. Also, most of us have observed members of the same family sitting around the table actively involved not with each other but with their individual cell phones or *iPads*.

Work schedules too can lead people to misplacing their love. I have been retired for two years and often get calls to substitute for a teacher. Even though JoAnn and I have made plans for the day, it's tempting to think I love my neighbor by going into work without discussing it with her. It takes an effort to stay the course and put those in my family first. There might be a time when going into work is more important, but I need to make that choice with the mutual agreement of the family.

When I got my first *iPad* I found learning how to use it took more time than I thought. What this all boils down to is making a choice to be fully present to those who are around us. Although the choice to ignore the things of the world is not an option in most families, the choice to put interacting with our family members ahead of the things of the world is something we can all do. In the interviews I had with many parents, a common thought was to watch out for those things that lure us away from focusing on each other. This vigilance can help our children balance their playing with interacting with their family. One thought that many voiced was the frequent temptation to use television programs and video games as a way for parents to have their children engaged in things that get them "out of their hair." It's true; we all need our "private time." However, it might be better to engage the children in things that are helpful and interactive rather than to allow them to spend time doing things that cause them to focus on themselves.

JoAnn and I found our "private time" in a planned way. Most days when I came home from work the first thing we did was to sit down, pour a glass of wine and spend 20 minutes talking about our day. If additional time was needed, we could wait until the children were in bed. Our children exercised great patience in respecting that time. This became "private time" for them as well. It is a small thing but those little things do count.

Setting goals *with* the members of the family can be a way to achieve ownership. Here the reader might consider these simple ideas as a beginning.

Every day we should spend some quality time together (not counting dinner). Never let a day go by without the children hearing the words, "I love you." Read a chapter together from their favorite book. Sit with them during homework sessions to talk about school and the concerns they may have. You will be surprised what comes out of these times together. Say night prayers together.

Take an active role in listening to one another without giving advice, unless it's asked for. Active listening involves leaning forward with eye contact. Acknowledging that you understand and if you don't, ask questions that help whoever is sharing to clarify without feeling threatened.

I remember my daughter at the age of five wanted to tell me something about her day while I was reading a book. She paused, reached up and gently took my chin and turned my head toward her. She understood from past modeling that it was important to have my full attention, which meant having eye contact. These little things do count.

Find a time to be one on one with each family member at least once a week. It doesn't have to be a lot of time but it's worth every minute.

Share the good things and the not so good things that went on during the day when you weren't together. Have you ever heard this in your conversations with your children?

Dad: "How did your day go?
Child: "Fine."
Dad: "Anything special happen today?
Child: "Nothing too much."

These kinds of conversations were so common for us when our family was young. However, when we, as parents, began to model what a good conversation could be like and we started to *listen with eye contact*, our children opened up.

After having these limited conversations with our children several times, JoAnn and I wondered how we could stimulate more of a dialogue at the dinner table. We were at a loss because we wanted our children to be free and not feel that they had to participate in a "tug of war" with us to get them to talk. I decided one day, to secretly record what happened during one of our meals. That night I played the recording to JoAnn. We both were amazed when nearly all we heard were the sound of dishes, silverware and chairs scooting around. Somewhere along the line, one of the children said something and got an "A-huh" from me. All the while, the clatter of knives cutting and forks stabbing went on.

Well that was the end of that conversation. I could just imagine that our child thought, "Well, he must not be interested in knowing more." It was clear what we had to do. We decided that beginning with our next meal together when anyone said something we would put our forks down and give our undivided attention to the person who had anything to say. At first it seemed awkward and strange. However, after a few days of this practice, it was amazing what we experienced. Everyone seemed to sense that what they had to say must be important and conversations began. What a simple, yet profound thing to do...give undivided attention to each other. That even meant extending our mealtime because we had to stop everything to listen. Food became secondary to putting each other first.

Another family had a unique way to create and encourage meaningful conversations at the mealtime:

Often, when we sat down, one of us parents was tempted to start asking questions to hear how the day went or what the kids still need to do for homework before going to bed. One night, we sat down, and we resisted this usual pattern. We said nothing. It was quite a unique experience. There is so much chatter in our lives during the day at work or school or other activities, that sitting down to eat in silence was just what we needed. After about five minutes of eating, one of our teenage daughters said something about school, and a discussion followed among all of us. It was a reminder to us that sometimes our children need to have some silent moments — even in the times that are usually thought of as "family communicating time."

Tuck your children into bed (yes, even those in high school) to generate an opportunity to talk a few minutes. I found this time to be a wonderful opportunity. I sat on the edge of the bed to just be present to each child.

We enjoyed this practice. When the children were young, we would sing a special lullaby. As they got older, we would sit on the end of their bed to talk over the day. We not only shared our day but also they shared concerns and joys of their day. We often left them with the feeling of thankfulness for those precious moments. Such a small effort on our part produced such wonderful results. The little things do count.

Find new ways to work together. We have a rule in our family: the cook never washes the dishes. When we started this, our son voluntarily began to help. Today he has this same habit with his young family. It really does amount to the fact that it's the little things that count in building a loving and caring atmosphere in the family.

I tend to look for those grand inspirations that will bring people together in greater harmony. I have become convinced that if I just take advantage of the opportunities to love in each moment, it will be little things that produce the best harmony.

Real-Life Story
Expecting Nothing in Return[6]

Saturday I had planned to work around the house to finish some long-delayed projects. I had even spent time figuring out the priority of each job. When I was just about to start, my sons dropped by and asked me if I wanted to play golf. I was tempted to tell them of my plans for the house, but this was a chance to spend some quality time with them. When we got to the first tee, the mosquitoes were making it impossible to concentrate on our game, and if we didn't do something about it, they were going to ruin the day for us. None of us had any repellent!

Here was another opportunity to love them. Without hesitation I wheeled the cart around and headed back to the clubhouse. By the time I got back, they had completed the first hole and were midway into the second. I told myself, "You have to love, expecting nothing in return." I had to repeat this phrase several times to fight my impulse to be upset because they had not waited. I jokingly told them that the first and second holes would probably be my lowest scores since I took a par for each of them.

The game went well, and we enjoyed our afternoon together. To my surprise one of my sons thanked me for having played with them, saying, "You always try to love us, and sometimes we take that for granted." Giving me a big hug, he said, "Dad, I want to be like you with my own children."

His remark gave me the certainty that no matter how small an act of love is, it always leaves a mark and makes a difference.

Step 3
Recognize the Value of Suffering and Conflict

But if we believe that behind the events of our lives there is God with his love, and if strengthened by this faith we can recognize in big and small daily sufferings, our own and those of others, a shadow of the crucified and forsaken Christ and our participation in the suffering that redeemed the world, it will be possible to understand the meaning of the most absurd situations and put them in perspective.

Chiara Lubich[7]

I WANT TO SHARE A secret that is the "Key" to perfecting and keeping harmony in the family. Since we are human we can only strive for perfection but we can take a big step towards that perfection by living in a family where harmony is the rule rather than the exception. It comes as no great surprise that family life will experience suffering and conflict. They are a condition of life and as hard as we try to avoid them, suffering and conflict come. These things occur in family life every day, and perhaps even many times a day. We experience conflict when we don't get our way. When things happen that we don't expect, we suffer. We have differences of opinion and differences in the way we express our feelings. Family members know all the "buttons" to push that can shatter the peace that was there only a few minutes before. The reason for this is that we tend to think only of ourselves. When this happens, we seldom have the other's best interest in our hearts. Those little things do get in the way. These are times when it is the most challenging to love the other person. Whenever a challenge like this comes, I am always faced with a choice: I can be upset and rant about it or I can embrace it and find a way to love through it.

Here are three suggestions that could be helpful when faced with suffering or conflict. These are secrets or keys to transforming the atmosphere of the family.

First, suffering is *always* valuable! This may be a difficult concept to swallow because most of the time we try to avoid suffering. However, when we face the reality that suffering or conflict is an inevitable part of the human condition the choice we have then is how to handle it. To embrace any suffering whether small or large is to always put the other in first place above the suffering. To illustrate this, I remember a time when we were going out of town:

> One of the family members was late getting home and that gave us a late start for the airport. The traffic was much heavier than usual and it soon became evident that we were going to miss our plane if traffic didn't break loose soon. The reality was we can be late for our flight and angry with the individual who contributed to our lateness or we can be late for our flight and love that person. Being late was not going to change. The choice was ours to make. It was simple. It was a time to put the family member first, ahead of missing our flight. We started a game we usually play while in the car. We actually did miss the flight but were able to get the next flight out and the best part of it all was the peace in the car was never lost. It was a valuable lesson for all of us to see the suffering as an opportunity to love each other. It was a

catalyst to continue developing a trusting and strong relationship.

We can always start out on the right foot in our approach to the suffering that naturally occurs in family life by accepting as a fact that suffering has value. This is where the "rubber meets the road." Whenever conflict occurs in our home, we try to approach it with this attitude. It is an opportunity to learn from and to grow in our love for one another. We certainly don't always succeed in looking at a situation as an opportunity, but we try every day to begin with the attitude that suffering has value. Whenever we manage to live this way we parents gain credibility with each other and with our children. More times than I would like to admit the issue had become more important than the person. I came to realize, however, that a simple reversal of this makes all the difference in the world. When we put the person in first place, we have a much better chance of looking at any suffering or conflict in a way that is empty of our own ego. It becomes a sort of contest to get on with the task of reestablishing our relationship after it has been broken. It is so much better that way!

Second, any conflict or suffering can be recognized and embraced *immediately*. We can't pause in this. This takes some practice. If we do pause, we are likely to be caught up in our own ego or our need to be "right."

> This has been difficult for me because I have a big ego! At times JoAnn asks me to drive in a way that is less aggressive. That has caused me to get my defense armor on because I look at it this way: she has no confidence in my driving. So, what's the problem? The problem is I put the need to be right over her concerns. Once I came to that conclusion, the decision to comply was easy and immediate.

Remembering that it is always best to put the person ahead of the issue immediately, we are more free to move ahead.

Finally, there is a certain *joy* when we embrace any suffering or conflict and we demonstrate our love by putting the person ahead of the issue. It's true that we experience fulfillment when we are in harmony with each other. When we are able to do this, our children learn that the best way to know joy for themselves is to try to look at conflict or suffering as an opportunity to grow. The experience of our trip to the airport, although small, was filled with the joy of loving one another because it was important to concretely model authentic love in the face of that small suffering.

Real-Life Story
Shopping with My Daughter[8]

When my daughter entered junior high, it became difficult for us to shop together for her clothes. She naturally became interested in the latest styles that her friends wore. But, I found myself reminding her of what was modest, practical and economical.

She dragged her feet through the mid-priced stores that I preferred. I frowned at the places she preferred. For a couple of seasons we went through many stores and most of the time we became discouraged and tired. Often we settled for something neither of us was happy with.

We both began to dread shopping. She thought that I didn't care about her concerns. She also thought that I treated her like a child. We shopped only if we had to, and then would find ourselves under the pressure of a deadline — and this made things even worse. I deeply regretted that we couldn't enjoy these times together. I knew there just had to be a better way.

Recently the dreaded plan to go shopping was upon us, but this time the Golden Rule came to my mind: "Do to others whatever you would have them do to you." I decided to do something to change things.

As we approached the mall I didn't head for my favorite stores. I asked her where to park, in order to be close to the stores she liked. She was surprised and happy at my new attitude! Inside the mall, I was peaceful. I assured her that I wanted to find something she would be truly happy to wear.

To my surprise, she chose a reasonably priced store. When I saw that she walked right past the sale rack, I didn't say anything. When she found something we both liked, I offered to try another store, just to be sure. But she was happy.

Then, I suggested we find one more thing. She smiled as if I offered her a gift! Again, she chose something we both could agree on. When we paid for the items, she saw that they were more expensive than usual. She looked at me with some doubt, but I assured her that I was happy that she had found something she really liked. I could sense she felt understood, and I had the clear impression that we had not undone any lessons in "economy." Rather, we had learned something about love.

Real-Life Story
Loving Through Pain and Discouragement[9]

Sometimes suffering can have the tendency to crush us. Our hope ebbs and desperation or even despair gets the best of us. However, with the right attitude and commitment, suffering can be transformative.

There can be many reasons for suffering in a family: an illness, the death of a loved one, a financial loss, etc. For us, in our family, it was the illness of our 15 year-old granddaughter, Caitlin, who was diagnosed with Crohn's Disease. One day she was rushed to the hospital in acute pain, and placed in Intensive Care. It was determined that she had a massive infection from a perforation in her intestine. It was a critical moment for her and our family and surgery was scheduled. When we went to see her, we weren't sure how we would find her, but when she saw us, she managed to give us a little smile and thank us for coming.

As time went on several complications occurred. For a while, it seemed like her health situation was never stable, and her time in the hospital seemed never ending. However, in spite of the many set-backs she and her parents incurred, they clearly focused on loving each person who came into her room. They tried to make her room a welcoming environment for her and anyone who came in to visit. They colorfully decorated the door and added a new verse from the gospel that they were trying to live that day. The flowers she received and the cards that were sent were prominently displayed for all to see.

The atmosphere in her hospital room, was like that in a family, a place where everyone felt loved and welcomed. In fact her doctors, nurses, and those taking care of her, would comment on how Caitlin would ask about them and thank them for all they were doing for her. Her surgeon would comment on her beautiful smile which lit up the room in spite of her pain. Caitlin would tell us, "I am in pain all of the time, and the only way I have found to get through it is to keep praying and to keep loving. That helps me to not focus on myself and what I'm going through. Rather, I want to focus on those who come to visit because I realize that they are probably suffering too because of me. I have so many people praying for me and this is what gets me through it all."

Watching our son and daughter-in-law live out each day, was for us a testimony to the beautiful unity between them and a witness to how a family can live and love through suffering. They put aside everything in order to help each other cope with the day to day struggles. Our son was the uplifting and motivating force while our daughter in law was the nurturing force. I never experienced friction between them because both understood the importance of being together and the role they must serve. It was a lesson in how to walk a walk united in the one purpose.

Step 4

Don't Be Self-Basting ... Reach Out

God created the family as a model for every other human coexistence. This therefore is the task of families: always to keep the fire of love burning in every home and to reawaken those values that God entrusted to the family in order to bring them generously and without rest to every sector of society.

Chiara Lubich[10]

*S*INCE WE HAVE FOCUSED on creating an atmosphere within the family of building trust and communication through "loving one another" "making the person more important than the issue," and embracing every suffering "always, immediately and with joy," we can now look at the outward expression of that love and see how serving others enhances family life even more. I usually don't speak in absolutes except I think I can say that every time we are able to forget ourselves and think of the other, we are *always* more fulfilled and happy. We have experienced this first hand not only in our lives but also in the lives of other families who practice reaching out to others. However, JoAnn and I have learned that we have to be careful how we do this in the context of family life.

I remember that a few years ago we got very involved in a project serving our church that took a lot of our time. We were convinced that so many people would benefit from the good we were doing that we committed much of our spare time to it. Our children knew what we were doing but had little part in it themselves. We found that members of our family were becoming like "ships in the night" and our interaction had seriously diminished. We often left our children with other families while we traveled.

We learned that it is important to remember that the needs of our family come first, because that *is* our vocation as parents. Connecting with each other through consistent and meaningful communication and being physically present is essential. We need to be available to share, to listen, to laugh and to enjoy the company of one another. The single most important thing in family life is to love to the point that each member feels that he or she is valued as well as united to the others in a way that no one should feel excluded or marginalized. Ideally, each one will put the good of the other before his or her desires. When we got so involved with the church, neither JoAnn nor I had considered how undertaking this project without the children's consent or involvement would impact the family as a whole. It was a fundamental mistake for us. I don't want to give the impression that a family must do everything together. On the contrary, a teen may go with a group to do community work while the parents go to a nursing home. These things are great if they are planned in an atmosphere of mutual agreement.

Another important aspect of serving is to share the experience with one another. This invites the support and interest of the other members of the family and encourages them to continue reaching out. Finding ways to serve others can be left up entirely to the creativity and culture of any given family.

Taking a look back at the activities many said were potentially harmful to building strong personal relationships within a family (see introduction), we have seen that families who lead a *balanced* life together and avoid these distractions, become beacons for many others. How do they do it? After interviewing several families, all with very different approaches to the way they live, I discovered that the "family needs" are as varied as there are families. However, a common thread that all have, seems to be the need to define family as "one in which everyone is involved in the process of communicating with one another." This means planning together, discovering together, and knowing the needs of the other. Sometimes, out of necessity, the needs of one or the other take priority. However, when the whole family has had some practice in paying attention to the needs of the others, this kind of necessity doesn't upset the balance because everyone can see the truth in the situation.

Here are a few examples of what some families are doing to avoid being self-basting and to become more outward looking.

A single parent

At the beginning of every month the family (two girls and mom) sit down with a big calendar that hangs on the refrigerator. They each write on the calendar their regularly scheduled appointments. For example, one might have music lessons; another will have karate while mom has a couple of meetings she needs to attend. After they place those things on the calendar, they discuss what they would like to do together and put those things on the calendar too. Of course, they admitted there are those times when it's necessary to have a little flexibility because something conflicts with their plans. This gives a reason to sit down together and decide what the priority is. They do it together. Part of the monthly conversation is planning one or two events where the entire family can serve others. For example, going to the Food Pantry to help sort food into meals, visiting a nursing facility to bring some joy to the elderly. Many times, it is something as simple as going to visit a neighbor with a cake or joining a faith community to help with an event. These are all good ways of reaching out.

Another family

They plan their evenings together around the dinner table. One thing that this family holds to is their agreement to complete all homework, phone calls, and business before they have dinner. They reserve their family activities for after dinner. They admit that there certainly are times when dinner is a little later than usual because some things had to be finished but they always discuss what has to be changed. Then, during mealtime, the family discusses what they could do during that month to serve others. Usually it is one thing a month, but it is always reaching out beyond the home into the hearts of others.

We realize that planning like this could be difficult for many families, especially families with older children, but we do think that planning is essential. Make the time and be creative. I personally can never say, "I don't have time to do something." What I do say though is, "I'll make time to do it." It's a matter of asking myself, "What is the priority?"

Real-Life Story
Sharing[11]

We try to teach our children an attitude of sharing with each other and with others. We have tried to lead them in this regard through modeling by sharing our own things.

For example, we have a garage sale box in our basement closet. We have a garage sale every year to help other families meet their needs. The children have noticed throughout the year that we put things in the box, that are quite nice. They decided to follow this practice and when they sort their things out, they often add some of their belongings to the box – to the point that we now have more children's items than adults', and the box is overflowing.

We see, on many occasions, that our children are the example for one another and for us. For example, we have encouraged our children to share the candy they received so it becomes the candy of the entire family. When our youngest child was four years old she found it difficult to accept this. She wanted to hold on to her own collection. However, seeing how her older brothers accepted this as being a good way of loving one another she too decided to share her goods.

Our family struggles with the almost overwhelming consumerism in our society. There are times when it might seem very important for our kids to have certain designer clothes or for them to want something that their friends might have. Sometimes, however, they surprise us by their generosity too. For example, one of our sons received two dollars from his grandfather on Christmas Eve. He had the money in his pocket during Mass. When it came time for the offering he put his two dollars in the collection basket. Interestingly enough, after our meal on Christmas day, my brother decided to treat this child to an instant lottery ticket. To my son's delight, he won two dollars.

As our children got older and started to earn money, we encouraged them to broaden their vision and think of other people's needs. Our son was a paper boy and after keeping a portion he earned for a little spending money he gave an equal portion of his earnings to a group of young people who were working on a project to assist poor families. He also heard about a soup kitchen in the city where his aunt works. He decided to give money for that as well.

Step 5

Learn from One Another

Parenthood is an important stage of a family's development. It is the birth and multiplication of new relationships, a phenomenon that will increase as the life of the family progresses. The family will become a treasure chest, a wonderful interweaving of relationships of love, of intimacy and of friendship: nuptial love among the spouses, maternal and paternal love toward the children, filial love toward the parents, brotherly and sisterly love among the children, love on the part of grandparents for their grandchildren and vice versa, for aunts and uncles, for cousins, for friends of the family, for neighbors.... God truly created the family as a mysterious jewel interlaced with love.

Chiara Lubich[12]

WRAP EVERYTHING, EVERYTHING, EVERYTHING in love. *Do what we do out of love for the other person. Try not to be self-serving.* This could easily be the motto for a family whose members strive to be in harmony. One of the most important things we have found in building strong relationships is the transparency we have achieved with one another. Hiding things such as thoughts, plans, and judgments is damaging to all relationships. Children need to know what priorities, intuitions, and feelings inform their parents' decision-making. Parents need to know where their children are coming from in terms of their fears, desires, intuitions, and feelings. This kind of understanding promotes honesty, integrity, empathy, balance, good listening and above all trust. We have tried to encourage our children to share not only their thoughts and ideas but also their feelings and responses to one another's actions. We have found that feelings held inside lead to judgments and judgments lead to divisions between the members of the family. As the experience below of the father who didn't trust his daughter's judgment illustrates, whenever we are judging, loving one another is not possible. Therefore, when we are transparent with one another, everything is out in the open. Even if something is painful, we can deal with it in ways that promote and encourage the family's growth.

Does this way of living sometimes lead to lively discussions? Of course it does. We have never shied away from a lively discussion, but we have, at least most of the time, come to a peaceful conclusion. When we remember to do everything out of love for the other, we discover that solutions are not far away. If parents share the stories of their own lives, both past and present, the children will learn to share their lives with each other and with their parents. We will have many more opportunities to know one another when we are transparent.

A family that I spoke to shared:

> Many times, when our children were growing up, we played a game called, "I remember when …" We told stories about our childhood and most of the time our children were so delighted that they asked us to repeat them again and again.

One more thing

Parents have to try hard to find ways to shut out the obvious distractions that surround them. All of us have to put those *iPhones* and *iPads* away, at least for short periods of time. We all can be guilty of letting the things of the world into our lives at the most inappropriate and disruptive times. We have to find time *every day* to quiet down just to be together and to be present to one another, even if it's only for a few moments. Parents can become leaders in this effort. It's great when family members no longer pass each other like ships in the night, but rather see each other like beacons of light.

Another way to help develop healthy relationships is to teach our children how to offer loving feedback to one another. We call it: "The moment of truth." As a gardener wants the plants and trees in his yard to be healthy, he prunes the unnecessary parts of the plant so it can grow strong and straight. Many times the parts he prunes are living but growing in such a way that the plant will not look good. Parents watch their children grow and sometimes must correct them lest they run into trouble. We are certain that parents would never allow their children to do things that might be life threatening. So why would we let the people we love grow in a way that might produce character flaws that would hinder social development, or perhaps cause them lose their way in life? It's very likely that the others see the flaws in us way before we see them ourselves. Hence, this is the moment to help each other grow straight.

Parents and children can do this. It just takes the appropriate atmosphere where a family gathers in openness and love for each other. This is not a time to bring tension and discord to the table. It might be wise to postpone it if anyone in the family is angry or upset. We recommend scheduling this during a time that is free from distractions so that everyone can be present to the others out of love for them. Here's a possible method.

Put everyone's name in a bowl. Choose someone to lead and oversee the discussion. (This person's responsibility is to watch carefully to be sure the atmosphere doesn't turn negative and counterproductive.) We recommend that one of the parents lead this for the first few times, so the model can be well established. As time goes on one of the older children could act as the facilitator. Pick a name from the bowl. This person becomes the focus.

Each member of the family says one good thing about that person (an admirable quality about that person, not "I like your shoes.") It could be something that person did to show sensitivity toward another. Then share one thing about that person that is keeping him or her from growing straight. It might be something that helps that person to be more patient or less reactive to the others. On the other hand, it may be something as simple as "I would love it if you shared your day with us at dinner instead of remaining silent.

This person listens carefully and doesn't offer any defense, even if what the others say may not be entirely accurate in that person's mind. Parents allow the children to say what they see for the chosen person's growth. It is surprising how perceptive they are when given the chance to share.

If there is time draw another name or wait until the next scheduled time. Perhaps this could be planned once a month.

May our families continue to grow closer within themselves and with other families so that we can become lights for the multitude of families who get lost in our dark world. Our lights are vital because the world yearns for direction.

Real-Life Story
My Daughter's Friend[13]

I am the father of seven daughters, and together with my wife, we have tried to maintain a spirit of mutual love in our family.... I really think they are beautiful girls ... so when something threatens them in my judgment, I sometimes react very strongly. Some would call this being overprotective, and I admit that I have been excessive in this regard. But, there is a lot to protect, and much to protect them from.

This can be illustrated in an experience I had over a period of time with one of my high school daughters. From the time she was in eighth grade, she seemed to be drifting into things that I found potentially damaging to her goodness. The music she preferred, the films and TV shows she would have watched, if I had allowed her, were indicative of this. She had a few friends that I thought had the same, tastes and I began to unconsciously judge them. This was especially true for one of them. In fact, she began talking and associating with this girl almost exclusively.

To make matters worse they attended the same high school. So things intensified. Little by little, I got more and more intolerant. There were times that I got very angry with her when she talked on the phone too long. I accused her of becoming "boy crazy." I knew I was wrong, but my feelings would get the best of me and I would say these things before I could control them.

I knew this was not love for her or for her friend. As much as I didn't want her to go in the wrong direction, I saw that I was sliding.

I learned through my faith that love excludes no one, but I was excluding my daughter's friend. I knew that I should love my "neighbor's" daughter as I would love my own. It wasn't a matter of feelings. It was a matter of love, a love that would be tough for me. I took a step, by asking my daughter to have her friend over. One time I even made the suggestion for her to stay overnight. When she came to our home, I asked my daughter's friend about her family and school. I tried to show a genuine interest in her family. During future visits, it seemed like she was feeling a little more comfortable and willing to come over. She still liked the kind of music that I found non-constructive, but I set that aside in order to maintain openness and communication. I still was not happy that my daughter spent so much time with this one friend. I tried to encourage her to spend time with others too. So when it was time for the annual father/daughters' dance at her school, I happily agreed to go.

My older daughter was going too, so we had it all planned and were ready. My daughter's friend wasn't going, because her father was out of town.... I realized that the best thing to do in order to love my daughter's friend as I would my own daughter was to invite her too to the dance. After all, her father was away and couldn't bring her, so I could fill in as her father.

That's what I did, and she came.

The dance was another exercise in loving. I'm not the dancing type, but decided to be as one with my daughter as I could. You would have thought I did this every week. At times, I was dancing with all three at one time. At a certain point, I danced with my daughter's friend. I told her, "Tonight you're my daughter." The moment came for pictures. I knew that, in the future, I could look at this picture of my two daughters with me and remember a beautiful experience, doing something that made them happy. However, when our turn came to pose, I insisted that the friend be part of the picture. She loved it, and I was even happier. Since then, things have been going well. I have gotten to know the friend better, and I learned that in some cases, I had really exaggerated my judgments about her. These judgments prevented me from loving her. Changing my attitude about the things she and my daughter liked, I've helped to create an atmosphere that helps my daughter to be a good influence on her friend.

Conclusion

It is my hope that these 5 short chapters have helped the reader reflect on some aspects that could lead to Great Parenting. In no way do I mean to suggest that this is the only way for families to grow closer. However, I do want to emphasize that the 5 elements above have been concretely tried and tested with wonderful results. I am grateful to God for giving us the wisdom to form each person in our family into wonderful loving human beings.

May all of us parents remember and put into practice these simple 5 steps:

1. Always love one another.

2. Make the little things count.

3. Recognize that suffering always has value.

4. Bring your family's love to others by reaching out.

5. Never stop learning from one another.

Through these 5 points we have discovered a depth and beauty in family life that we didn't experience before.

Notes

1. *Essential Writings: Spirituality, Dialogue, Culture*, p.185. New York and London: New City Press, 2007.

2. *Essential Writings: Spirituality, Dialogue, Culture*, p. 183.

3. As shared by Mary Black.

4. As shared by JoAnn Rowley.

5. Unpublished address given by Anna Maria and Danilo Zanzucchi, on January 23, 1998, at Volunteers Convention held in Castel Gandolfo, Italy.

6. As shared by Tom Rowley.

7. *Essential Writings: Spirituality, Dialogue, Culture*, p. 191.

8. As shared by J.M.

9. Shared by Tom Rowley— not previously published.

10. *Essential Writings: Spirituality, Dialogue, Culture*, p. 191.

11. As shared by L. & P. W.

12. *Essential Writings: Spirituality, Dialogue, Culture*, p. 187.

13. As shared by Len Szczesniak.

New City Press
of the Focolare
Hyde Park, New York

New City Press is one of more than 20 publishing houses sponsored by the Focolare, a movement founded by Chiara Lubich to help bring about the realization of Jesus' prayer: "That all may be one" (John 17:21). In view of that goal, New City Press publishes books and resources that enrich the lives of people and help all to strive toward the unity of the entire human family. We are a member of the Association of Catholic Publishers.

Other Books in the 5 Step Series
www.NewCityPress.com

5 Steps to Effective Student Leadership	978-1-56548-509-9	$4.95
5 Steps to Living Christian Unity	978-1-56548-501-3	$4.95
5 Steps to Facing Suffering	978-1-56548-502-0	$4.95
5 Steps to To Positive Political Dialogue	978-1-56548-507-5	$4.95

Scan to join our mailing list for discounts and promotions

Periodicals
Living City Magazine, www.livingcitymagazine.com